GREAT YA[

and GORLESTON

The Past Fifty Years

Compiled by
Colin Tooke

First Published 1998
by
Tookes Books
14 Hurrell Road
Caister-on-Sea
Great Yarmouth   NR30 5XG

ISBN 0 9532953 0 3

Printed in England by Blackwell John Buckle
Charles Street, Great Yarmouth, Norfolk

Introduction

The town of Great Yarmouth has changed considerably in the past fifty years. This book looks at some of the changes since the end of the Second World War but by its size cannot give a complete picture of the changing townscape, particularly in the 1950's and 1970's when many areas of the town were cleared and redeveloped.

Following the end of the Second World War in 1945 the town set about restoring its position as a leading seaside holiday resort and making a serious effort to alleviate the chronic housing shortage which the war had created. The clearance of old property unfit for human habitation (which had begun before the war) and the repair and replacement of houses damaged or destroyed during the war was hampered by a severe shortage of labour while the return to the town of many evacuees and the release of personnel from the services made the task all the more urgent. In the following ten years many areas of the town were to change almost beyond recognition as new buildings were completed and new roads laid out. Unfortunately this post-war enthusiasm for rebuilding meant that much of the old historic town was swept away, no consideration being given to saving even a small part of medieval Yarmouth and the unique 'Row' system of town planning was lost forever. This decision may have been influenced by a comment made in a report for post-war reconstruction drawn up in 1943 when the Planning Officer stated "the Rows contain few examples of buildings of architectural merit or historic interest..."

The townscape we know today was principally formed during two separate periods of redevelopment, the first in the 1950's when the ravages of the war years were cleared away and the second in the early 1970's when the town centre (Market Gates) was developed together with a new road system on North Quay and through the centre of the town (Temple Road).

The holiday industry was soon bringing top line entertainers to the town during the period that was to be the heyday of the British seaside resort, the period from the mid 1950's to the end of the 1960's. Industry expanded during the same period bringing a new lease of life to the south end of the town as large factories such as Erie Resistor and Birds Eye developed, together with many smaller firms.

These, with the other main employers in the town such as Grouts silk factory, Johnsons clothing factories and Smiths Potato Crisp factory provided work for many thousands of people. Timber imports resumed but after a brief post war revival the fishing industry went into decline in the early 1960's until it finally died out altogether. A new industry, North Sea oil and gas exploration, rapidly developed to become the main port activity and fill the gap left by the fishing industry. The town was successful in attracting new industry but the decision to locate this on the South Denes, where access was to become difficult, was in retrospect not such a good idea.

Oranges washed ashore in the week before Christmas 1948.
This cargo of oranges was one of the first shipments sent to this country after the war, intended for allocation in the north of England. The ship carrying them, the *Bosphorus* bound for Hull, grounded on the Happisburgh sands and had to jettison her cargo to float free. A north-east wind brought the cargo ashore along the beaches north of Yarmouth and provided a surprise Christmas bonus for local people, many children having never seen an orange.

The Immediate Post War Years

In 1943 the Town Planning Officer's report on the reconstruction of the Borough was far reaching and, had it been fully implemented, Great Yarmouth would have had a very different townscape today. New road schemes formed an important part of the plan, the Acle Road to enter the town over a high level bridge crossing both the river and North Quay to the summit of Fullers Hill (which was then still a hill) to form "a wonderful entrance to the town". The road was to cross Northgate Street at a large roundabout and continue to the Regent Road/Nelson Road junction to give the motorist a direct route to the Marine Parade. The main road entering the town from the north, taking the line of Caister Road and Northgate Street to the above mentioned roundabout was to continue along the line of Howard Street to another roundabout situated between Broad Row and Regent Street. From here new roads west to Hall Quay and east to the Nelson Road junction would be constructed. A third river crossing to link Main Cross Road with Gorleston Baker Street, either by bridge or tunnel was proposed and many of the remaining roads in the Borough were to be widened or re-aligned. A yacht station "with all modern facilities" at the north end of the town and an airport between Gorleston and Lowestoft were also envisaged. Only small parts of this report were implemented however when the post war redevelopment began in the early 1950's.

Among the important developments that were commenced in the late 1940's was the establishment of an estate of temporary houses (prefabs) at Shrublands, Gorleston and a large estate of permanent houses on the Magdalen College lands, also at Gorleston. On the Shrublands estate a total of 711 prefabricated houses were erected, the largest such estate in the country. The first prefabs were ready for occupation in 1946 and although intended only as temporary homes parts of the estate lasted for many years. At the northern end of Great Yarmouth it was planned to extend the North Denes Estate and complete the Jellicoe Bridge over the railway, building of which had been suspended during the war years.

Industrial development on the South Denes began with Hartman Brothers of London being among the first companies to lease land for a new factory (today Tenneco Packaging). A new Erie

Resistor factory opened making components for the radio and defence industries and Birds Eye Foods moved into the town, producing frozen food in their new factory for the first time in 1946. The fishing industry still accounted for much of the land use on the South Denes and this came back into use as the fishing season recommenced. Part of the sea-front area of the South Denes was given over to holiday use as a tent camp. Caravans soon began to replace tents and the camp expanded to accommodate over 1000 holiday makers, the caravans later extending to the main denes area as far south as the Harbour Mouth. In other parts of the town Grouts silk factory in St. Nicholas Road (now the site of Sainsburys) and Johnsons clothing factories changed from war time production to a wider range of consumer goods and in 1948 Johnsons opened a new factory on the corner of North Quay and the Conge, mainly for the production of overalls.

The holiday industry emerged from the closures imposed during the war years and although rationing still existed for food, fuel and clothes the summer season brought holiday makers to the town again in 1946. The fuel restrictions and lack of private car ownership meant most holiday makers travelled by coach or train, the town until the end of the 1950's having three railway stations, Vauxhall, Beach and Southtown which together coped with a huge influx of people determined to put the war behind them and enjoy at least one weeks holiday at the seaside. By August 1946 the beach from the Harbour Mouth to Caister Lifeboat Shed was declared free of all mines, as was Gorleston beach. The Gem changed its name to the Windmill Theatre and opened in June 1946, featuring twice nightly variety shows with an almost unknown name, Norman Wisdom, on the bill. The Pat Collins Pleasure Beach reopened after six years and other attractions such as the Waterways, Marina open-air theatre, Bathing Pools and the Winter Gardens all came to life again.

In 1948 a new motor sport was introduced to the town when the 'Yarmouth Bloaters' speedway team was established at the Caister Road Stadium, which until then had only been used for greyhound racing. This new attraction drew a crowd of several thousand people to the track every Tuesday evening from April to October.

The sea front illuminations were reinstated in 1949 following the war time blackout, leading the town into a brighter decade during which many changes were to take place.

NEW BRITANNIA PIER

OCEAN BALLROOM

VICTOR SILVESTER

will present

FOR YOUR DANCING PLEASURE, YOUR

Favourite Radio Orchestras

A Different Star Band Every Week

❖ ❖ ❖ ❖

OCEAN RESTAURANT

Menus to serve all tastes

Works and Factory Outings a Speciality

Accommodation for 1,000

BUFFET SERVICE and FULLY LICENSED BARS

❖ ❖ ❖ ❖

PAVILION THEATRE

NIGHTLY DURING THE SEASON

The New "HAPPIDROME"

THE FAVOURITE FAMILY RADIO SHOW

with the original Comedy Stars

MR. LOVEJOY   RAMSBOTTOM   ENOCH

CELEBRITY CONCERTS EVERY SUNDAY

The Britannia Pier summer season for 1948.
In the days before television it was the radio stars of the day who provided the big names for seaside entertainment. Among the stars to appear at the Sunday concerts in 1948 were Arthur Askey, Richard Murdoch and George Formby. The Ocean Ballroom and Pavilion Theatre on the Britannia Pier were destroyed by fire on 20 April 1954.

The 1948 Yarmouth Bloaters' speedway team.
Left to right: Reg Morgan, Max Pearce, Dick Wise (Manager), Roy Duke,
Paddy Hammond, Bill Carruthers, Sid Hipperson, Billy Bales,
Bert and Ted Rawlinson.

Billy Bales (left) was the youngest rider in the Bloaters team and his daredevil riding made him a firm favourite among the supporters.

The first Speedway meeting at the Caister Road Stadium was held on 20 April 1948 when 16 riders competed for the East Coast Trophy, eventually won by Bert Rawlinson.

A crowd of 4000 attended this meeting, swelling to over 10,000 in successive years. The speedway finished after the 1953 season, was revived in 1957 but finally ended in 1961, to be replaced by Stock Car racing.

German prisoners-of-war preparing the 60 acre site at Shrublands before the prefabs were delivered. Each house was delivered in four parts and bolted together on site. *(Picture courtesy Eastern Counties Newspapers)*

Once completed Shrublands was the largest prefab estate in the country. The weekly rent was 12s 6d (62p) for a home complete with bathroom, fitted kitchen and refrigerator, far ahead of its time. Each had its own small garden as can be seen in this picture of a completed part of the estate.
(Picture courtesy Eastern Counties Newspapers)

This aerial view of the town centre taken c1949 shows the destruction caused by the 1941 air raids in the Middlegate area where at least 300 houses were left unfit for habitation and numerous businesses destroyed in one night. Part of the area has been cleared but many bomb damaged properties remain, both in the old 'Row' area and along South Quay. Yarmouth Way was constructed across the open space in the centre of the picture and the remaining damaged properties removed in the early 1950's as flats replaced the old row houses.

At the top of the picture is the Parish Church, burnt out by incendiary bombs in the early hours of 25 June 1942. Between Arnolds Department Store (the building with the white pillars) and the Regal Cinema (the large building on the far right of the picture) is an open area where the Marks & Spencer store was destroyed in 1941 together with many other shops in King Street including Kerridges, Halfords, Maypole Dairy and Hills Restaurant.

The Fifties

By 1950 almost 2000 families had been rehoused on the new Magdalen College estate at Gorleston and reconstruction of the war damaged town centre began with clearance orders being issued for the southern part of the old 'Row' area between King Street and the South Quay. New blocks of three and six storey flats were built and a new road, Nottingham Way, was constructed. The first blocks of houses were ready for occupation in November 1952 and the redevelopment continued northwards, in stages, for the remainder of the decade. Yarmouth Way was built in 1954, this requiring the demolition of Docwras Sweet Factory and the old Middlegate Street from here to Nottingham Way was widened and renamed Tolhouse Street. A new Unitarian Church opened in 1955 to replace the one destroyed in the war and restoration work began on the Tolhouse. From Yarmouth Way to Hall Plain the old Middlegate Street became Greyfriars Way.

Redevelopment further north involved the Howard Street and George Street areas between the Market Place and the North Quay where again blocks of flats replaced the old row houses. Another new road was built, St. Francis Way, which necessitated the demolition of the town mortuary on North Quay.

Rebuilding had taken place in King Street and in 1952 the new Marks & Spencer store opened, the firm moving out of their temporary home in the old Plaza cinema in the Market Place. Six years later the cinema was demolished and a new Woolworth store built on the site. Also in the Market Place the Angel Hotel was demolished in 1957, replaced the following year by new shops which today include Dixons and the Halifax.

A major development on the South Denes was the construction of the power station which opened in 1958 after four years building work. The chimney reached to a height of 360 feet to become the second highest structure in the county, a landmark seen from miles around. Commercial use of the South Denes continued to grow and a Herring Reduction Factory was built to turn any surplus herring into fertiliser. This was in anticipation of the expansion of the herring industry which unfortunately did not happen and the factory closed after only a few years in operation and was then demolished.

As far as the holiday industry was concerned the Circus was reopened by Billy Russell (the last of the summer venues to reopen after war time closure), a new children's amusement park, Joyland, was built to the south of Britannia Pier and artists appearing in the summer shows included names such as Tommy Trinder, Eddie Calvert, Derek Roy and George Formby. Pleasure flights started from the Caister Road airfield. In Regent Road the House of Wax opened in 1955 and the previous year the Victoria Hotel, opposite the Wellington Pier, was renamed the Carlton.

At the north end of the town caravans appeared for the first time on the North Denes, land that had been earmarked for houses and hotels a few years earlier. A new school, North Denes Junior, was opened to serve the increasing population in the north of the town.

In 1953 disaster struck the town in the form of devastating floods. Nine people lost their lives, thousands were rendered homeless and extensive damage caused when the town was attacked on two sides by the worst flooding in living memory, part of a chain of disasters which swept down the east coast following a lethal combination of high spring tides and northerly gale force winds on the night of Saturday 31 January. The first flooding came shortly after 8pm, two hours before normal high tide. The sea flooded the Marine Parade causing considerable damage to the Jetty and other buildings while the overflowing river flooded many homes in the Blackfriars Road area and at Gorleston. Later that night the banks of Breydon Water broke in several places leaving flood water several feet deep in Southtown and Cobholm, long after the water had subsided in other parts of the town. Over 20,000 sandbags were needed to effect a temporary repair to the banks of Breydon.

Thousands of people were evacuated to places like the Caister and Gorleston Holiday Camps as the Council emergency committee began to organise relief. Blankets, clothes and food were quickly brought into the town and in the days following the disaster fire pumps from the Midlands joined Army and RAF personnel in an effort to reduce water levels and dry out houses.

The town recovered from the floods in time to celebrate the Coronation on 2 June 1953. The day, although wet, was celebrated in the town with a salute of 21 guns by the 1st East Anglian Regiment from the Marine Parade, an athletic meeting at the Wellesley, a carnival procession which included Yarmouth and Gorleston, a river spectacle and dances at the Floral Hall (now the Ocean Rooms), the Winter Gardens and the Ocean Ballroom (on the Britannia Pier and burnt down the following year). Official decorations on Marine Parade stretched from the Britannia Pier to the Pleasure Beach with others on Hall Quay and the Town Hall and Upper Marine Parade at Gorleston. All school children in the town were given commemorative mugs and a copy of the New Testament while pensioners were given a quarter of a pound of tea (in a commemorative packet) and free entrance to the Circus and Little Theatre.

During the 1950's the town received its first regular television service, from the BBC in 1955 followed by ITV in 1959. Television created a new home leisure activity and way of life for many people, the cinemas being among the first to notice a dramatic change in peoples lifestyles.

In 1953 a new bridge was opened over the river Bure to replace the hundred year old Suspension Bridge. Although intended as a temporary structure this bridge was to remain until the early 1970s despite the congestion caused by the almost right angled approach and exit road on the North Quay side. The Breydon Swing Bridge was closed to rail traffic in 1953 and the swing section left permanently in the open position until the whole structure was demolished in 1962. In 1956 steam trains were replaced by new diesel rail cars on the Norwich line and the following year the push-pull steam engines were replaced on the Lowestoft line from Southtown station. Holiday traffic on the railways reached its peak during the period 1958-1961. On each summer Saturday in 1958 no less that 40 express trains originated from the town to all parts of the country. In 1959 one of the towns three railway stations closed with the pre Beeching cuts to the ex-M&GN line from Yarmouth Beach station to the Midlands. The last day of service was 28 February and track removal started within a few weeks, the site of the Beach station being bought by the Corporation, part to be used for housing, part for a new Coach Station.

Average earnings for a male manual worker in 1959 were £13.2s.11d (£13.15) per week, a new bungalow could be purchased for £1,475, an average family spent £1.8s.1d (£1.40) per week on food and a new 'mini' car cost £500. During the decade many new words, such as 'teenager', 'teddy boy', 'transistor radio', and 'traffic warden' were added to the English language. The fifties were over and the town was now poised to move into the 'swinging sixties'.

The 'Yarmouth Follies' was the Windmill show for 1950 seen here in the Carnival of that year. The proceeds from the first performance were given by Jack Jay to the newly formed Yarmouth & Gorleston Publicity Association.

The Marine Parade outside the Marina Theatre in the summer of 1954.

Scots fisher girls packing herring into boxes for John Woodger & Sons. By the 1950's the Herring Industry Board had been established, as marked on the boxes.

A drifter unloading its catch in the 1950's. The fish are being unloaded into boxes on the lorry rather than swill baskets used in the pre-war years. In the background is the Gorleston Gas Works on Southtown Road.

The Coronation carnival procession 2 June 1953 entering Hall Quay from Regent Street. The Five Smith Brothers were appearing at the Windmill Theatre for the season. Also in the procession can be seen the 'Corporation' open top Coronation bus.

The Joyland children's amusements next to the Britannia Pier opened in 1951 and the 'Ark' seen here was built the following year. This picture was taken during the Coronation procession as above

Aerial view of North Quay and Fullers Hill 1953.

In the above picture, to the left, is Rainbow Corner which led into Rainbow Square, today the site of the Post Office sorting office. The white building in Rainbow Corner is the factory of 'Rainbow Ices', manufacturers of ice cream until 1956. On North Quay opposite the bridge is the North Tower public house and the Lacon's Brewery complex can be seen to the centre right of the picture.

The buildings seen in the foreground and those on Fullers Hill were all demolished in the early 1970's when the new bridge over the river Bure was constructed to replace the Calender Hamilton bridge seen at the bottom of the picture. This bridge, seen under construction in the smaller picture was opened on 5 January 1953 to replace the unsafe suspension bridge of 1847 which can just be seen on the right. Although only intended to be a temporary bridge it was to remain in place for almost twenty years.

Flooding on North Quay, 1 February 1953. In the background is St. Andrews
church and school, now the site of Comet electrical showrooms. The buildings
on the left were demolished when the new bridge was built in the early 1970's
and today a car park occupies the site on the corner of Fullers Hill.

Local residents surveying the aftermath of the 1953 floods in Blackfriars
Road waiting for the water to subside before the big clean up could begin.
This picture is taken from the SE tower looking south. Charles Street came
through to Blackfriars Road where the advertising boards are on the right.

Litchfield Road, Southtown, 1 February 1953. Residents of many houses in Southtown and Cobholm had to retreat to upper floors as the flood waters rose to a depth exceeding three feet in many places. The water took many days to subside in this part of the town before the slow process of drying out the houses could begin.

Boats of all shapes and sizes, many from the seafront boating lakes, were used to rescue people and take supplies to those stranded in their houses immediately after the flood.

By June 1955 redevelopment was well under way in Middlegate, new
properties covering much of the old' row' area of the town.
(Picture courtesy Eastern Counties Newspapers)

King Street in 1954 before Yarmouth Way was cut through between St.
Georges Rooms and Frere & Co. the wine merchants.

Regent Road on a busy day in the mid 1950's. Many of the buildings in this picture have now been demolished, on the right is the Electric House, demolished to make way for the Market Gates development in 1974 and behind that the Regal Theatre demolished in 1989. In the centre of the picture is Divers public house demolished in 1978.

Regent Road in the mid 1950's. The Woolworth store closed in 1959 when the company moved into their new store in the Market Place, the site of the old Plaza cinema which had been the temporary shop for Marks & Spencer until 1952. Curry's cycle and radio shop moved to the Market Place in 1978.

Today the Billiard & Snooker Hall (opened in 1925) is above KFC and McDonalds.

The vehicle registration EX seen on the car in the foreground was exclusively issued to vehicles registered in the town from 1904. In 1956 it was replaced by three letters (AEX) and in 1974 ceased to be an exclusive Yarmouth registration.

King Street c1955. On the left is Matthes Restaurant, above the shops. Male's chemist shop later became a branch of the Co-op. On the right is the small shop of Montague Burton the tailors, 22 King Street, which later became Mansfield's shoe shop. Cycle bags and baskets can be seen in the doorway of Halfords

Fifty Shilling Tailors at 20 King Street later changed its name to John Colliers Ltd. Halfords, offering "£1 deposit secures any cycle" moved from here to Market Gates in the 1970's. The van belongs to Bessey & Palmer a local fuel merchant whose office was in King Street, almost where this photograph was taken from.

A 1954 view of the roundabout at the eastern end of Regent Road with the Queen's Hotel (now the New Beach) in the background. Hazel's Restaurant is on the opposite side of Regent Road. This was the year when the Pavilion and Ballroom on the Britannia Pier were destroyed by fire in April and the summer show, Ted Ray and Hylda Baker in "You Can't Help Laughing", was transferred to the Aquarium Theatre.

The Seagull 'mini' coach outside the Britannia Terrace booking office, seen here decorated for the 1953 Coronation.
This unusual advertising vehicle was a familiar sight driving along the Marine Parade in the 50's and 60's.

A diesel railcar from Lowestoft approaches the platform at Southtown Station on 30 July 1958 while a B17 class steam locomotive 'Liverpool' prepares to leave.

A busy scene on Hall Quay in August 1959 as a Birds Eye train of frozen food containers makes its way along the quay tramway to the factory on South Denes, causing considerable traffic congestion. This rail link from Vauxhall station to the south end of the town was finally closed in 1976.

Cleaners and shed staff at Yarmouth Beach station in 1956.

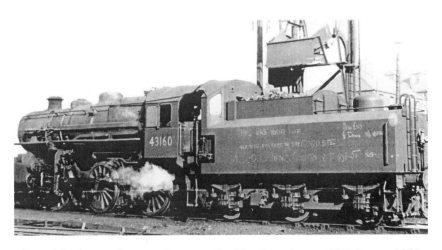

One of the last engines to take on coal at Beach station on 28 February 1959.
The line to the Midlands closed at midnight that day, the site soon to be
turned into a coach park. Beach station had opened in 1877 and was the
terminus of the M&GN line, for many years dubbed the 'Muddle and
Go Nowhere' railway.

Coaches arriving in the town in July 1957 when Church Plain was used
as the main coach park.
(Picture Courtesy Eastern Counties Newspapers)

Whit Monday, May 1959. Norwich day trippers arriving at Vauxhall station.
(Picture Courtesy Eastern Counties Newspapers)

August 1959, the production lines at Erie Resistor factory on the South Denes making electronic components for the radio, television and defense industries.
(Picture Courtesy Eastern Counties Newspapers)

The 'Green Bean' production line at Birds Eye Foods August 1959.
(Picture Courtesy Eastern Counties Newspapers)

This picture, September 1954, shows the church before restoration work began and Fullers Hill before the 1970's demolition. In the right background is the silk factory of Grout & Company, now the site of Sainsbury's supermarket.

Gorleston open air swimming pool in 1953. Opened in 1939 with the adjacent Floral Hall the pool was a popular amenity until it was recently demolished amid many protests from local residents. The site of the pool is now a garden.

The Sixties

As the town moved into the nineteen sixties the majority of post war housing development had been completed in the town centre and at Gorleston. In 1961 work started on a large development of private houses at the north end of the town, the Peddars Cross estate.

The fishing industry declined rapidly at the beginning of the decade until no Scots drifters travelled south for the fishing season and Bloomfield's, one of the major firms in the Yarmouth fishing industry, sold its famous 'Ocean' fleet of drifters in 1963. Land on the South Denes was used for other industries and Erie Resistor expanded over part of the area previously used by Bloomfield's. Birds Eye built a new cold store in 1961 and doubled its size only four years later. Goods traffic leaving Yarmouth by rail reached its peak in 1962 when 24,500 containers of frozen foods from Birds Eye and pulp products from Hartman Fibre left the town using the quay tramway to Vauxhall station.

Coincidental with the demise of the fishing industry was the increased activity in the North Sea search for oil. The first test well was commenced on Boxing Day 1964 by the drilling rig Mr. Capp and four months later a drilling ship Glomar IV began work 50 miles off the Norfolk coast, the first to be serviced from the port of Great Yarmouth. Wimpey/Brown & Root established a base in the town and they were quickly to be followed by other companies connected with the North Sea operations. Bristow Helicopters provided the essential helicopter services to the rigs, using the North Denes airfield to establish a Heliport. Port facilities expanded to accommodate the new industry, quays were repaired and buildings that had been used for the fishing industry were either altered or demolished and new warehouses and sheds were erected. Oil exploration led to the discovery of gas in large quantities and by the late 1960's Yarmouth had become the largest offshore marine base in Europe, supporting 27 rigs working in the North Sea.

In the town centre the library moved from its temporary home on Hall Quay to a new building at the rear of the restored Tolhouse in 1961 and the parish church of St. Nicholas was reconsecrated following a long period of rebuilding. New bells had been cast from those damaged in the war and once again rang out over the town.

One of the ABC Sunday shows in 1965, featuring a young Tom Jones. Top seat price 9/6 (47p). The main summer shows for that year featured Norman Vaughan and Joe Brown at the Britannia, Mike and Bernie Winters at the Wellington, Lonnie Donegan at the Aquarium, Jimmy Wheeler and Alan Smethurst (the Singing Postman) at the Windmill and The Bachelors at the ABC Theatre.

Major changes took place in the late 1960's at the White Horse/Beccles Road junction when the traffic lights were replaced by a roundabout. A lot of property was demolished to widen the road junction including these cottages on the north-west corner.

A new police headquarters was opened in Howard Street by the Home Secretary in 1963 to replace the temporary premises at 26/27 South Quay that had served as the towns police station since 1947. Five years later the town lost its own police force as the Yarmouth police merged with those in other parts of Norfolk to become part of the Norfolk Joint Police Authority.

Seaside holidays were now at their peak, the old Beach railway station was first used as a Coach Station in 1961 and among the many entertainers to visit the town during the sixties were Tommy Steele, Frankie Howard, Billy Fury, Rolf Harris, Engelbert Humperdinck and Tom Jones, many of these just beginning their careers in showbusiness.

In 1964 the Blue Anchor public house on the west side of the Market Place, on the corner of the Conge, was demolished and a new building erected for the Westminster Bank while on the east side a new store was built for Tesco (now a newsagents and Argos). On the Marine Parade the Coastguard Station was demolished to make way for the Tower leisure complex which incorporated the town's first ice skating rink on the ground floor, now used as an indoor market. The Vauxhall caravan park opened to cater for the ever increasing need for holiday caravans in the area. Rebuilding started on the Gorleston breakwater which meant the end of the popular 'cosies', as the sheltered niches on the south side of the Dutch pier were known, and the demolition of the familiar coastguard lookout and lighthouse at the end of the pier. The town narrowly escaped a major disaster in 1964 when an American jet fighter crashed on Darbys Hard at Gorleston, the pilot ejecting and landing in Lawn Avenue.

In 1966 Whitbread's acquired control of Lacon's the local brewery and two years later announced they were to cease brewing in the town. The closure of the brewery on Church Plain was a bitter blow and 150 workers were made redundant. The brewery buildings were to stand empty for a few years before being demolished in the early 1970's. In 1969 Arnolds department store in King Street celebrated their centenary, selling Ice Diamond refrigerators for 46 guineas (£48.30), prams for £21 and television sets for 60 guineas (£63.00). Shop assistants could now earn £7/10/0 (£7.50) per week and Camplings Laundry offered evening shift workers 5/- (25p) an hour. A three bedroom house in Newtown could be purchased for £4250.

The 'cosies' on the south side of the old harbour south pier with the lookout and lighthouse at the end of the pier. Many timbers in this pier dated from the original construction of the 16th century. The pier was rebuilt in 1964.

All set for a broads trip on the *Resolute* and *Queen of the Broads* while the *Golden Galleon* is already on her way. Havenbridge House (built 1973) now stands on the quayside where the Steward & Patteson offices can be seen. In the background is the box factory of R. H. Porter Ltd.

The open Haven Bridge disrupts traffic on Hall Quay as a coaster makes her way up river in the 1960's. Goods trucks wait on the sidings for a train to take them along the tramway to the South Denes.

In 1967 the temporary Shrublands prefab estate was demolished to make way for more substantial housing, although many people were unhappy to leave their homes where they had lived for twenty years.

(Picture courtesy Eastern Counties Newspapers)

The 'Big Star Show' of 1962.
The three Vernons Girls with Billy Fury (on the right), Karl Denver (centre)
and Marty Wilde (left). Below: the audience enjoying the show at the Windmill
Theatre. (Note the 60s hairstyles of the younger members of the audience.)

The opening night of 'Secombe Here' at the Wellington Pier 1 June 1962. Also in the picture are Ronnie Corbett, Lonnie Donegan, Terry Hall and Yana.

A sixteen year old Helen Shapiro on the Pleasure Beach go-carts. The 'Helen Shapiro Show' was at the Royal Aquarium in 1963.

A British Railways three wheel vehicle with a container of egg boxes ready to leave the Hartman Fibre factory in the 1960's. In the background is a pile of waste paper awaiting treatment and the recently opened power station. These three wheel traction units were used by the railway for local delivery from rail terminus to customer premises.

The 'Round House' near the Lower Ferry which was demolished in April 1967. Built in 1912 this was the first herring sale ring and had been unused for many years when this picture was taken in 1966.

Lacons Brewery as seen from Church Plain just before its closure in the late 1960's. After the demolition of the brewery premises the present Tesco supermarket was built on the site.

Through the gate was the 'brewery yard', seen here just after the closure of the brewery in 1968.

Overill's cycle shop and Savory's warehouse in the Market Place were demolished in 1964 to build a new Tesco store. Overills cycle shop had been established in 1913.

The Tesco store built on the site of the above shops in the Market Place. The posters in the windows advertise Green Shield Stamps which could be exchanged for a wide variety of goods in the Green Shield showroom at Norwich or by catalogue. Today Argos occupy part of the building seen here and both Penthouse and the East Wind Restaurant have gone.

The Market Place as it looked in the late 1960's. Pedestrianisation had been considered but no action was taken for several years. At this time traffic followed a clockwise route around the Market. Tesco's new store can be seen on the right hand side.

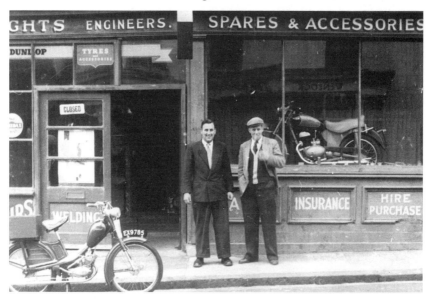

Motor scooters and mopeds were a popular form of transport in the 60's. At 40 Fullers Hill was the motor cycle shop of Clarke & Knights which later in the decade became a secondhand furniture store.

The SW Tower, part of the town's medieval defenses. Through the passage in the base of the tower can be seen the shops in Blackfriars Road.

This view of the rear of the SE Tower taken in June 1969 from Trinity Place shows the Ironworks of Batley & Parmenter, built against the town wall.

It was because many houses and other properties had been built against the wall during the latter part of the nineteenth century that the wall survived. The wall in the Blackfriars Road area was cleared of such buildings in the early 70's. The tower in this picture later became a small museum, part of the Pottery which still adjoins it in Trinity Place.

Blackfriars Road looking north towards the Victoria Gardens public house c1960. On the right is the shop that a few years earlier had been William Philpot, Chemist, on the corner of Abyssinia Road.

In the mid 1960's Gregory Gedge, saddler, was on the south side of Friars Lane, now the site of the Fire Station. Also on this side of the Lane, between Garden Lane and the South Quay was the office and works of Stanley Bird, basketmaker, Ellis's fish and chip shop and the Clipper Schooner public house. A passage led to Adam & Eve gardens at the rear of the above properties.

On the corner of Friars Lane and South Quay is Yarmouth Stores, general outfitters, founded in 1898 on this site as a ship chandlers. This picture c1965 shows the shop before the rebuilding and modernisation in the mid 1970's The ship chandlers and sail loft of Yarmouth Stores are situated further south in Southgates Road.

South Quay c1960. On the corner of Mariners Road is the Tudor Cafe and behind that the First & Last public house, demolished in 1989 and now the site of a car sales yard. The First & Last was so named because it was either the first or the last public house (depending on the direction of travel) for people entering the old town through the South Gate of the medieval town wall which stood across the road at this point (the site marked today by the end of the wall seen in front of the public house). In the background is Drury House, an Elizabethan property, demolished in 1969 following much controversy over its preservation, claimed to be the finest example of a house of that period in the town. The only part to be saved was the fine staircase which went to Blickling Hall.

The Seventies

Throughout the seventies there were more large scale developments in the town, both in new road systems and new buildings, than had taken place since the post war rebuilding programme of the fifties. In 1971 houses and shops in Fullers Hill were demolished as the road was widened and levelled. A new bridge over the river Bure was opened in March 1972 leading to the 'new look' Fullers Hill which was now no longer a hill. In conjunction with this scheme to provide an improved entrance to the town from the west a new road system on North Quay linked with Lawn Avenue on the eastern side of the White Swan public house. The previous road had passed between the river and the public house.

Fullers Hill was to continue as the 'Market Relief Road' across Church Plain and virtually eliminate Priory Plain, sweeping round behind the Market to eventually join with Alexandra Road. This necessitated demolition of many buildings including the Methodist Temple on Priory Plain which gave its name to the new road, Temple Road. Work also began at the southern end of the town with the demolition of many houses in Blackfriars Road and the surrounding area. Small houses which had relied on the medieval town wall for support since the early 19th century were razed to the ground to leave an open space against the wall while new blocks of houses and flats were built where Boreham, Clarence, Louise and Abyssinia Roads had been.

This period of demolition and change was not confined to Yarmouth. In Gorleston the Coliseum cinema in the High Street closed in 1970 and was demolished shortly after to make way for new shops (one of which is now Iceland) and in 1973 the Gorleston Holiday Camp, which had opened in 1937, was closed and two years later work started on a new housing estate, Elmhurst Court, which was soon to cover the site. The gas holders were taken down on the site of the Gorleston Gas Works on Southtown Road. This plant had stopped producing coal gas in 1965 when North Sea gas was brought to the town. A new chapter house was added to the Gorleston parish church in 1970 and the following year the shopping precinct was opened in the High Street.

Also in 1972 the new fire station was opened in Friars Lane, the first industrial units were built on the Harfrey's Farm estate, the Royal Aquarium was renamed Cinema One after extensive internal alterations and Arnolds department store, on the corner of King Street and Regent Street, was renamed Debenhams (to eventually close in 1985).

In 1973 a new office block, Haven Bridge House, was built on North Quay on the site of the office and store of the Norwich brewing company Steward and Patteson. The town's now defunct local brewery, Lacons on Church Plain, was demolished and the Corporation restored the fabric of St. George's church in preparation to open it as an Arts Centre. The construction of the Market Gates shopping precinct and car park began 1973. This involved the demolition of many buildings during the following two years including Fish Street and Jubilee Place, the Electric House in Regent Road and the Conservative Club in Theatre Plain. Two years later the new multi-story car park was completed and Sainsburys moved into the shopping precinct as the 'anchor' store.

The administration of the town came in for radical changes on 1 April 1974. Until that date Yarmouth was a County Borough Council, one of the few places in the country to hold such a status but this had to change with Local Government reorganization and the Town Council became a District Council, many of its previous powers being taken over by Norfolk County Council. Several rural parishes were taken into the new authority from the old Flegg and Lothingland areas giving the Borough a population of over 70,000 people. Services such as education, police, libraries, roads and social services were now run from Norwich and the towns Blue Buses extended their routes into the rural areas previously only served by Eastern Counties buses. A new Royal Charter gave the newly formed district the status of a Borough enabling the position of a Mayor to be retained.

More development began on the North Quay in 1976 when the remaining properties in Laughing Image Corner and Rainbow Square were demolished in preparation for the building of a new Post Office sorting office, which opened the following year. The rail line from Vauxhall Station along North Quay to the old Fishwarf area was closed and the following year Southtown Station, unused since 1970, was demolished in preparation for the construction of Pasteur Road. The oil and gas industry had now firmly established the town as a supply base for its North Sea operations and rig supply boats had become a common sight in the port, as were the Norfolk Line roll on-roll off ferries Duke of Holland and Duke of Norfolk.

In 1977 new legislation allowed local authorities to run their own lotteries and Great Yarmouth was one which took up the option. A kiosk at the southern end of the Market Place sold the 25p tickets for the weekly draw. The Prime Minister of the day, James Callaghan, made a rare ministerial visit to the town in May to speak to the conference of the Transport and Salaried Staff Association held at the Britannia Pier. It was in the seventies that inflation began to take a stronger hold on the country and between 1971 and 1978 pay packets almost trebled as did many prices, coffee rose from 28$^1/_2$p to £1 for a 4oz jar, cigarettes went from 31p to 70p and a bottle of brandy from £3.35 to £6.35 .

The 70's ended as they had begun with more demolition, this time on the Marine Parade where in 1979 the Marina open air theatre and the adjacent swimming pool were knocked down to make way for a new indoor sports complex, the Marina Centre.

The southern end of the Market Place May 1971. New decimal coinage had just been introduced and the chip stalls are selling chips at
4p, 5p and 6p per portion.

Guests being presented to H.R.H Princess Margaret outside the Town Hall by the mayor, Alderman Kenneth Hammerton on 24 June 1970. The Princess was entertained at the Town Hall for lunch following a visit to the Parish Church and Birds Eye Foods.

1974 entertainment at the open air swimming pool, Marine Parade.

The west side of the Market place in May 1971. The sunblinds on the shop next to Palmers (extreme left) are outside Purdy's the confectioners which was to close the following year. (Now the Halifax Building Society)

Purdy's Kenya Coffee Room was on the first floor, with access through to Palmers. When the Kenya Bar closed Palmers opened their new coffee room. The large sunblind is on Coopers shop (see page 46).

Downs Supermarket, seen here in 1971, was renamed Downsway in 1973. From 1976 until 1979 it was Fine Fare Supermarket and today is Mackays clothes shop.

Coopers electrical and furnishing shop at 32 Market Place in December 1974. The Ironmongers shops were in Market Row and North Market Road. The following year the Market Place shop became Norfolk Radio, later changing to its present name of Hughes.

Coopers Gorleston shop in the High Street, December 1971. To the right is Boots and Lipton's (now Iceland) on the site of the old Coliseum Cinema.

Barnes the grocers on the corner of the Conge and Market Place closed in January 1971 and later the shop became Claxton's clothes shop. The clock now on the side wall of Claxton's was salvaged from the Central Arcade when it was refurbished as the Victoria Arcade in 1987.

The Igloo Food Centre, 42 King Street, was the town's first frozen food shop, opened in 1972. In the window the shop is advertising 5lb of frozen peas for 66p and cod or haddock at 15p per pound. Today this is Kings Wine Bar.

The Easter Fair, April 1971, on Church Plain with the closed brewery
buildings in the background.

Sideshows at the Easter Fair on the Market Place in 1971. To see the Mickey
Mouse Circus cost 4p and the Ape Man 5p.

Nichols Restaurant in the Market Place, May 1971, when a large cod and chips cost 25p. All this property was demolished for the Market Gates development.

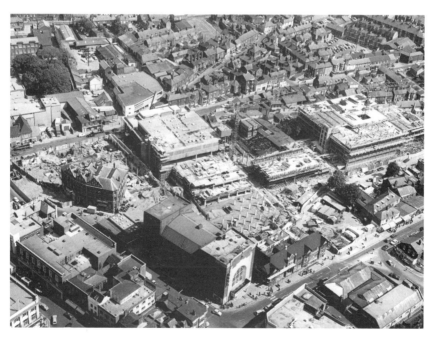

The Market Gates construction well under way in June 1974.

The Coliseum cinema in Gorleston High Street closed in 1970 and was demolished the same year. The shop on the left is Coopers the ironmongers.

Gorleston Holiday Camp was opened in 1937 and closed in 1973. Demolition began two years later when the housing development of Elmhurst Court was commenced.

The Yare Hotel on Hall Quay closed in May 1974 and five years later the Midland Bank moved into the building. Watneys Red Barrel was a popular beer of the 70s. The Yare was a popular venue in the 50s and 60s for American Servicemen from nearby air bases when on leave in the town.

Another of the towns public houses named after a local river was the Bure Hotel on Caister Road, seen here in 1977. This closed in 1986 and was quickly demolished to make way for new houses.

The ABC summer show for 1979 (above) was 'Holiday Startime' featuring the Bachelors and Beverley Rainbow, three daughters of the singing group the Beverley Sisters (two of Joy's daughters and the other Teddie's daughter). Also in the show were Billy Dainty and an almost unknown name, Michael Barrymore.

The 1975 ABC show featured the comedian Dick Emery. Seat prices for this show were £1.40, £1.20 and £1 for seats in the stalls and £1.40 to 80p for circle seats.

The Eighties and Beyond

Unlike the previous decade of demolition and rebuilding the eighties saw relatively little change to the townscape. The site of Lacons brewery on Church Plain had been cleared, a large archaeological excavation had taken place to find out more about the origins of the town and a new supermarket for Tesco built on the site. In 1980 the new store was opened by Russ Abbot, appearing in the town for the summer season. Other shops in the town continued to change and in 1985 Debenhams closed their large department store on the corner of King Street and Regent Street, the building being partly demolished and smaller shops opening on the site. A newcomer to the town that year was McDonalds, opening a fast food outlet in Regent Road.

Industry in the town was in decline, many of the large employers closing down or moving out of the town. Watney's maltings in Southtown were demolished in 1982 and the Smiths Crisp factory on Caister Road was closed in 1983 (demolished two years later). Erie Resistors large electronics factory on the South Denes had been divided into smaller companies and Birds Eye Foods, which had for several years been one of the town's main employers, closed their Yarmouth factory and moved all production to Lowestoft in 1986. The Power Station had closed down the previous year as had Palgrave Brown timber yards on Southtown Road. The timber trade was now almost non existent and the port relied on the activities of the North Sea oil and gas companies.

The summer season was now several weeks shorter than it had been in the fifties and sixties and there were fewer shows and big name entertainers. The pattern of the British seaside holiday had changed and many hotels and guest houses were put up for sale. A new all year round facility, designed for both local people and visitors, the Marina Centre, opened in 1981. Other places of entertainment were either renamed or changed their use. Cinema One became the Royalty in 1984 while the Regent Cinema was converted into a Bingo Hall and in 1987 the ABC cinema was renamed the Cannon. A new venture in the town, a floating public house, opened in 1983 aboard the Celtic Surveyor, a converted Shetland Islands ferry moored at Hall Quay. This enterprise was to have a short life however and closed the following year after the boat was arrested by the Port & Haven Commissioners for non payment of harbour dues.

A new hospital for the district, the James Paget Hospital, opened at Gorleston in 1982 and two years later the old hospital which had stood in Deneside for almost one hundred years was demolished and work started on a new housing complex, St George's Court. A new telephone exchange opened on North Quay in 1984 on the site of Rampart Road maltings and Laughing Image Corner and this brought six figure telephone numbers and new technology to the town.

On 1 August 1985 Her Majesty Queen Elizabeth II visited the town, arriving by train at Vauxhall Station. The royal visit was to included the Town Hall, Nelson's Monument, a walkabout in the Market Place, a visit to the Fishermen's Hospital and finally the Parish Church. There had been five previous visits to the town by members of the Royal family in the fifty years covered by the book.

1954 - The Duke of Edinburgh opened the Oriel High School.

1960 - The Duke paid a private visit to Birds Eye Food factory.

1970 - Princess Margaret visited the church and Birds Eye.

1972 - The Duke of Kent visited the Erie Resistor factory.

1979 - The Duke of Edinburgh visited Trinity House.

On 20 May 1993 the Royal Yacht Britannia moored off the town and the Queen was brought ashore in the Royal Barge to Stonecutters Quay where she transferred to a waiting car to take her to an official engagement in Thetford, to open the new Breckland Council Offices.

A new road scheme which was to have a big impact on traffic in the town, the Western Bypass, opened in 1986. This was designed to relieve the town centre congestion, the new road bridge carrying the by-pass over Breydon Water taking almost the same line as the old railway swing bridge of the 1950's.

Palmers department store, now the only department store left in the town, celebrated its 150th anniversary in 1987 and the following year work began to pedestrianise the Market Place in an attempt to improve the area for shoppers and bring trade back to the centre of the town. The recession was already being felt however and many small shops were closing. Sainsbury's moved out of the Market Gates shopping precinct in 1989 into a new store in St. Nicholas Road, built on the site of Grout's silk factory and out of town shopping superstores such as MFI and Halfords opened on the new Gapton Hall Retail Park in 1990. A new block of town centre shops opened on the site of the Cannon cinema in Theatre Plain and work continued on pedestrianisation of the Market Place, officially opened five years later in September 1995.

Among the properties demolished in 1990 were the International High School, previously the St. Louis Convent school, on North Drive, the East Anglian school at Gorleston, the Park Baptist Chapel in Crown Road and the Vauxhall Gardens public house. During the nineties there were notable changes to public houses in the town including the Gunner on South Beach Parade which was converted into the Rok Bar (June 1996) and the Wrestlers on Church Plain, famed for its Nelson associations, renamed Hardy's in February 1993. In 1997 however this changed back to its original name of the Wrestlers.

The ancient office of Mayor was abolished by the Council in January 1991, the last councillor to hold this position being William Dougal. This was the year work started on the Gorleston by-pass, a £16 million scheme to take through traffic out of the centre of Gorleston. The new road was opposed by many Gorleston people and caused the destruction of many houses along its route. It was completed in September 1993. In January 1992 the new Court House on North Quay, which had cost £3.16 million to build, was opened by the Duke of Gloucester and the same year a new Job Centre opened on the Conge. St. Nicholas hospital finally closed its doors to patients in 1993 and was put up for sale. After standing empty for three years a developer began work to convert the property into 62 houses and apartments.

Two new retail companies moved into the town in 1994 when Wilkinsons took over the empty shop in the Market Gates shopping centre that had been Sainsbury's and Lidl opened a supermarket on the Gapton Hall Retail Park. A disastrous fire in Market Row, the worst peace time blaze in the town in living memory, destroyed several shops on the night of Wednesday 13 September 1995. Over 100 firefighters tackled the fire and although council officers predicted it would take up to three years before the buildings rose from the ashes, at the time of writing this book much of the area is still in ruins.

The Crisp factory on Caister Road in 1985, two years after production was stopped and the year before it was demolished. Today houses stand on the site of the factory and the Bure Hotel, which can be seen on the far left of the picture, on the west side of Caister Road.

The Bath Hotel, Marine Parade, March 1987, when it was called the Circus Tavern with the Jugglers Bar on the St. Peters Road end. The ground floor of this building was later to be converted into the Flamingo Amusement Arcade.

The garage of Sidegate Motors, St. Georges Road in 1987. The business began in Sidegate Road on 1981 and moved to St. Georges Road two years later. In 1991 it moved to the Gapton Hall Industrial Estate and houses now stand on this corner site with Nelson Road.

The Park Baptist Tabernacle in Crown Road in 1989. The following year the chapel was demolished and a new one built further back on the site with houses fronting Crown Road. The original chapel had been built on this site in 1863.

Robin Askwith and girls from the summer show 'Further Confessions of a Window Cleaner' outside the Windmill Theatre on 5 July 1980. Local window cleaners had been invited as guests for a champagne reception on this night.

Russ Abbot at the Bradwell Scout Fete 28 June 1980 where he was made an honorary member. Russ was appearing in 'Showtime 80' at the Britannia Theatre with The Black Abbots.

Her Majesty the Queen paid a royal visit to the town on 1 August 1985, accompanied by H.R.H The Duke of Edinburgh. The visit began at 10.10am when the Queen arrived at Vauxhall Station to be greeted by the Lord Lieutenant of Norfolk, Mr. Timothy Colman and then proceeded to the Town Hall to be received by the Mayor Councillor J. Benson J.P.

The Royal Procession later proceeded to the Nelson Monument at the south end of the town and from there via Marine Parade to the Market Place, arriving at 11.30am. The Queen walked through the Market Place (above) to the Fishermen's Hospital where she was presented to the coxswains of the Great Yarmouth and Gorleston Lifeboat and the Caister Volunteer Rescue Service (all Honorary Freemen of the Borough). After a short visit to the Parish Church the Royal Party left the town by road.

This was the first visit to the town by a reigning monarch for almost seventy years. King George V had paid a brief visit to the Royal Naval Air Station on the South Denes in April 1916 as Admiral of the Fleet.

(Picture courtesy Eastern Counties Newspapers)

In the early hours of Wednesday 13 September 1995 a devastating fire tore through several shops at the western end of Market Row. This was the worst peace time blaze in the town in living memory, estimated to have reached 1000F at its height. More than 100 firefighters, some from as far afield as Lowestoft and Mundesley battled to contain the fire for many hours. The fire began in Courts furniture shop and quickly spread to the shops of Greenacres Butchers, Hubble Bubble and Hand Made Crafts all of which were completely destroyed. Other premises damaged included Bretts Furnishings, Collectables, Lasers Clothes and two empty shops.

Although the Courts store was built as recently as the 1960's the adjacent buildings were much older, including one built in the mid 18th century.

This had been the third blaze in the Rows in three years. In October 1993 a major fire in Broad Row started in Plattens outfitters and spread to adjoining shops and in July 1992 fire destroyed Dale's clothes shop in Market Row.

(Pictures Courtesy Eastern Counties Newspapers)

Bank Holiday Monday, 5 May 1997. The South Denes Power Station is reduced to a pile of rubble by a double explosion, the first destroying the turbine house and bunkers and the second a few minutes later bringing down the 3500 ton, 360 foot high chimney. A crowd of several thousand had gathered on the Gorleston side of the river for the 6am spectacular which was the culmination of three years demolition work by Tony Cox Dismantlers. For 23 years the power station had supplied electricity to the National Grid and was brought back into use during the miners strike of 1984 when the station ran flat out, breaking its previous generating records. A new gas fired power station is soon to be built on the same South Denes site.

(Picture courtesy Eastern Counties Newspapers)

Conclusion

Having reached this page in the book the reader should have, in a short time, passed through fifty years in the life of Great Yarmouth and Gorleston. The pictures and text have hopefully captured some of the interesting events and changes that have taken place during this period. This was a period when the town, in common with the rest of the country, saw a recovery from the austere conditions of the Second World War through the boom periods of the fifties and sixties to the more uncertain seventies and eighties. At the end of the nineties Great Yarmouth will move into its second millennium and Gorleston its third, who can foretell what changes will take place over the next fifty years. Future historians will no doubt capture these changes although whether photographs and the written word will be used in preference to more advanced communication systems remains to be seen. One thing that is certain however is that history will continue to be made and someone will capture it for future generations.

Acknowledgments

Many people have supplied photographs, information and advice for inclusion in this book. I would like to thank Peter Allard, Keith Blackwell, Peter Jones, Alec McEwen, Tony Overill and John Taylor for photographs from their collections and John McBride for access to his unpublished work 'Diary of Gt Yarmouth'. Eastern Counties Newspapers are thanked for giving me permission to use photographs taken by their staff photographers over the years.

My ever patient wife Jan has endured many hours of sorting through photographs and helping me to decide which pictures to include. Without her help and encouragement the book would not have reached the printers. This is the first book to be published under the name 'Tookes Books' and is a joint venture which would not have happened had Jan not been the driving force behind it.